W9-CHR-994

Contents

Where's Mom? She always meets Sam after school.

Sam holds his teacher's hand. She will wait with him until Mom comes.

Who meets you after school?

4

Here's Mom. "Hello Sam!"
Mom is sorry for being late.
She's glad Sam's teacher looked after him.
Miss Smith never lets children go off alone.

Sam has seen that man at the gate before.
He doesn't know whose dad he is.

But what a beautiful puppy!
"Can we stroke the puppy, Mom?"

"You shouldn't trust a strange dog, Sam.
You can't tell what dogs or people are like
until you know them."

Mom and Sam go back to tell
Miss Smith about the man.

Who do you
feel safe with?

"Why can't I trust that man?"
asks Sam.

"Most grown-ups wouldn't
hurt a child. But you can't be
sure about strangers. Some
grown-ups can be bullies."

"Stay with those you feel safe with," says Mom.
"Like Miss Smith and Maria's mom," says Sam.
"Or Dad or Grandma."

"Always tell one of us where you are going,"
says Mom.

The next day the man is there again.
At lunchtime Tina says, "I'm going to
ask that man if I can stroke the puppy."

Sam tries to stop her.

Tina knows she mustn't go
outside the gates.

What is she doing?

Tina really wants to stroke the puppy.
It looks so sweet.

But Tina wishes she wasn't alone.
After all, she doesn't know the man.

Tina looks back to where all her friends are playing.

She decides to run back to the schoolyard where she feels safe.

Where is a safe place to play?

13

Tina nearly knocks Miss Smith over.

"Come on, Tina. Let's go back into school."

The man with the puppy gets into his car.
He drives away quickly.

Tina is glad he has gone. She was right
to decide not to talk to the stranger.

15

Miss Smith talks to the children.

"People might pretend that your mom has sent them to pick you up. They might have other ways of tricking you."

Never take a ride from a stranger.

How can strangers trick you?

"It's best to go straight to someone you know."

"But you can stand up for yourself.
It's OK to say 'No' to a grown-up.
A caring grown-up won't mind at all."

Showing you a puppy...

Buying you an ice cream...

Giving you candy...

When Mom collects Sam from school
the man isn't there.
"Tina wanted to stroke the puppy," says Sam.
"But she didn't trust the man and came back."

18

Sam says, "I wouldn't talk to a stranger. If he tried to make me go in his car I'd shout NO! I DON'T KNOW YOU! and walk away."

"That's right, Sam." says Mom.

Don't talk to strangers!

At bedtime Mom hugs the children,
"So what have you learned today?"

"Don't go with strangers," says Jenny.
"Stay where you feel safe," says Sam.

20

Dad's home. "Can I have a hug?"

"Something happened today, Dad," says Sam.
"Come on then, Sam. Tell me all about it while I put you to bed."

21

waiting for Mom

asking
questions

telling the
teacher

deciding

feeling safe

saying
"NO"

23

Index

Find out more

Find out more about being careful with strangers at:

www.usa.safekids.org
www.pollyklaas.org
www.missingkids.com
www.safechild.org